Keying Into Something

Acrostics
of
Edith Blake

Wider Perspectives Publishing ¤ Hampton Roads, Va. ¤ 2021

All writings herein are property of Edith Blake and are creations of herself, all rights reserved to author/holder. Wider Perspectives Publishing reserves 1st run of printing rights, but all materials revert to property of the author at time of delivery. All rights to republication of items inside thereafter revert to the author and she may parcel items to contests and anthologies at will. No reproduction of this book, in part or whole, may occur without the permission of the author.

Copyright © Edith Blake, September 2021,
Wider Perspectives Publishing, Norfolk, Virginia
ISBN: 978-1-952773-40-2

Dedication

To Jack Callan and Judith Stevens,
friends and fellow poets who have been there in
difficult times and encouraging me to step out and
try new things. In others words to be
Brave **O**pen **L**earn **D**are.

Contents

Pandemic   1
Thoughts that have helped get through the 2020-21 pandemic, a time of great challenges.

Religious   11
Faith has helped and lifted me over the years.

Miscellany   25
… but not miniscule, these things fill our lives.

Motivation   39
Inspired by a number of sources like friends, Weight Watchers, improving health and making life work.

Nature, Animals & People   53
… swirls around me, gets me through, captures my attention.

Keying Into Something

PANDEMIC

Toilet Paper

Trusting in God to see us through
Onward together fighting this disease
In spite of restrictions hanging in there
Leaning on each other for encouragement
Easing into a new normal
Taking control of our lives

Pursuing our needs
According to situation finding ways to meet
Planning ways to keep entertained
Enduring the stress created
Rising above all the chaos

Panic

Patience in stressful times
Anticipate new challenges
Nurture others to find their gifts
Instill hope in us and others
Courage to step out in faith

Blake

Weapons

Working to eradicate the disease
Eliminating spread
Arming ourselves
Protecting loved ones
Obeying the edicts issued
Normalizing our new way of life
Supporting those who need help

Hand Sanitizer

Help in keeping us safe
Actively killing germs
Necessary when soap not available
Dependable way to clean hands

Safe alternate to use
Antibiotic liquid soap
Nonsense cleaning vehicle
Initiating safety precautions
Thereafter being clean and safe
Impressive at what it can do
Zapping germs and disease
Eclipsing risk of germs surviving
Reducing chance of getting sick

Virus

Victory in Jesus
Instilling hope
Reaching out to others
Uniting us as one
Shaping new life

Quarantine

Quiet our souls
Unite us as one in you
Around our faith
Raise our hopes
Awareness of the unknown
Normalize our fears
Tolerate our unbelief
Initiate trust in you
Nourish our growth
Everyone in this together

Corona Virus

Comforting to know His presence
Ordering our steps in serving Him
Raining down His blessings on us
Obeying His words in our actions
Naming our sins and misdeeds
Accepting His grace and forgiveness

Viewing others through his eyes
Involving ourselves in helping those in need
Realizing His greatness and love
Using our time wisely
Sharing our talents with others

Masks

Modern means of protection
Affirmative way to stop germs
Safety precautions during this pandemic
Key to preventing spread of disease
Symbol that people care for others

Blake

Solitude

Shaped by the feelings of loneliness
Oiled by the sense of uniqueness
Lifted by the hope for the future
Interested by the thoughtful thinking
Tuned into the sounds of the day
Unnerved by the silence broken
Disturbed by the loud noises
Eased back by the quietness of the moment

Keying Into Something

Religious

Prayers

Praise and thanksgiving
Rising from our lips
Aware of our needs and wants
Yielding our will to Yahweh
Encouraged by his words
Raising our voices as one
Single minded in our hopes and dreams

Renewal

Reenergized to become better
Encouraged to spread the Good News
Nurtured in His word
Engaged in ministry
Warmed by His grace
Accepted as we are
Loved beyond measure

Illumination

Inspired to create joy
Light the path to Christ
Love one another
United as one
Made from the heart
Invest your time
Nurture sense of purpose
Act for those less fortunate
Tell the Good News
Instill the love of God
Open yourself to hear God's call
Nourish your soul

Blessing

Believe all things possible
Listen for His voice
Encourage one another
Strive to be better
Serve with joy
Identify how you can help
Notice those around you
Grow in faith

Blake

Praise

Ponder the word of God
Ready to help
Alert to God's calling
Include not exclude
Strong in heart and soul
Envision what you can do

Good Soil

God with us at all times
Open to his word and directions
Onward we march doing his bidding
Doing good deeds for those in need

Seeds to grow in faith and grace
Other people focused not on self
Include all of God's creation in right living
Live in peace in God's world
                             and with each other

Hope

Hasten to see Jesus
Observe the season
Promise of joy to come
Expectation of the Lord's birth

Prepare

Present in each moment
Reveal God's will
Earnest in seeking God
Perceive what God is doing
Aware of God's call for us
Ready for his coming
Effective in serving and caring

Love

Long for His presence to comfort
Openness to seek His will
Value yourself
Envision God's plan for you

Peace

Power to overcome adversity
Enable to be at best instead of worst
Assurance that all will be okay
Courage to face troubles
Even in tough situations God is in control

Pivot

Putting trust on God's leading
Investing in learning more
Venturing into new challenges
Opening ears to hear God's words
Thanking God for His love and care

Discipleship

Devoted to living right
Inclusive of all people
Service to those in need
Change will happen
Involved in using gifts and talents
Pleased to do God's call
Longing for his guidance
Evidence of serving him
Sharing the good news
Holy and mighty is our God
Inspired by his love
Present in his presence

Cross

Christ in us
Rose from the grave
Obliterated our sin
Sacrificed for our lives
Smoothed our way to Christ

Keying Into Something

MISCELLANY

Grief

Growing in accepting a loss
Recognizing a sense of loneliness
Investing in ways to move on
Emerging stronger on the other side
Feeling better able to move on

Thursday

Time to look forward
Heeding one's beliefs
Urge others to enjoy life
Ready for the weekend
Stability for the week
Dreaming of future plans
Aware of new desires
You doing your own thing

Poetry

Praise and thanksgiving
Open to the spirit's moving
Expression of feelings and special moments
Treasures of memories
Random thoughts in words put together
Ying and yang of words

Friends

Forging relationships that last
Relating stories to let other know you
Including people in important celebrations
Extending helping hands to those in need
Noticing when someone is hurting
Displaying care for other's feelings
Sharing times together in fellowship

Dreams

Driving for an outcome
Reaching for the stars
Engaging in actions to attain goals
Aspiring to be a better person
Maintaining hope in times of hardship
Sustaining our efforts to remain calm
                                                in chaos

Tenacity

Testing our strength to last
Enduring through hard times
Negotiating ways to work change
Adapting to new ways of life
Creating new habits
Imagining a better looking self
Tasting the achievement of a goal
Yearning for desired outcomes

Strong

Strength to endure hardships
Tenacity in tough situations
Robust in dealing with problems
Obstacles easily overcome
Nobly enduring loss
Great in our reliance on prayer

Resilience

Recover from illness or loss
Energy to move to a better place
Sense of well being
Intellect in how to power through
Labor to move ahead
Inspire to be healthier you
Ease into a new normal
Nimble in understanding reason for feelings
Cheerful in midst of sadness
Embark on a new way of life

Wisdom

Willingly accepting knowledge
Insightfully becoming aware of change
Smartly learning new lessons
Daringly stepping out
Only working for the good
Mindfully seeking guidance

Courage

Caring for friends and family
Opening our hearts
Unceasing in reaching out
Reacting positively to change
Arising to the needs of others
Going the extra mile
Emerging with a sense of hope

Purpose

Point of doing something whole-heartedly
Unity in achieving goals
Resolve to better oneself
Ponder new changes
Objective in seeing both sides
Sureness of goals and outcomes
Endurance to work through hard times

Listening

Learning to hear what people say
Inviting people to share their opinions
Sensing the needs of others
Touching people's lives by caring
Encouraging others to open up
Nurturing people to grow in faith
Increasing wisdom in God's word
Noticing when someone is hurting
Growing in hearing the Spirit's calling

Blake

MOTIVATION

Strength

Strong as an ox
Tough as nails
Resilient when change occurs
Endurance to last
Navigate hard times
Gentle like a lamb
Transform in God's grace
Hopeful for the future

Connection

Concern about others in need
Open to ways to reach out
Nurture by God's word
Notice when people need help
Enable others to grow in faith
Celebrate God's healing hand
Trust in your abilities
Instill hope in others
Other people oriented
Negotiate differences in people

Focus

Figuring what needs to be important
Opening up to things that need changing
Chasing away unclear thoughts
Using skills learned wisely
Sharing with others our time

Change

Conquer hard challenges
Honor different opinions
Adapt to new ways
Navigate troubles waters
Grow in dealing with problems
Extend a hand to help

Division
a Positive View

Develop ways to unite as one
Inclusive of all no matter how you look
Value everyone for who they are
Influence perception of right and wrong
Source to affect change in ideology
Instill positive concepts and attitudes
Occasion for reconciliation between people
Nurture a sense of well-being for all

Advocate

Addressing needs of those in need
Developing ways to help others
Voicing for those who don't have a voice
Opening our hearts in concern
Caring for those we love
Arguing on behalf of friends and family
Treating others with respect
Engaging in sharing love and peace

Guidance

Gifts to be used wisely
Unique direction for our lives
Ideals to strive for
Directions to follow
Accept that change is necessary
Nurture natural talents
Clear path to follow
Envision new possibilities

Doubt
a Positive View

Doing away with fear
Opening your heart
Urging self to let go
Banning negative thoughts
Trusting in yourself

Goals

Give yourself something to achieve
Occasions for doing good for yourself
Aims for better living
Learn new habits for a healthier you
Special rewards for achieving end results

Unity

Understand that working together is possible
Nurture sense of one in purpose
Invest in equality and justice for all
Tend to the needs of those less fortunate
Yearn to not see differences but sameness

Commit

Consign yourself to do and be better
Open self to accept that change happens
Manage feelings in difficult situations
Maintain desire, pledge to a course
Include others to help you make decisions
Trust that your decisions are right

Success

Sustaining lasting results
Using talents to help others
Conquering hard challenges
Celebrating accomplishments
Emerging better off when change happens
Soliciting others for comfort during loss
Striving to improve one's self

Blake

Nature, Animals, & People

Cats

Creatures with their own minds
Affectionate beyond belief
Tangible means of love
Sassy and curious

Benny

Brightness amid darkness
Energy to spare
Noisy to a fault
Nice but naughty at times
Yielding to no one

Blake

Dogs

Dependable friend
Other people oriented
Good natured and caring
Strong and reliable

Breeze

Breath of fresh air to enjoy
Rustling leaves swaying back and forth
Energy flowing into surroundings
Earth's gentle reminder of nature
Zestful refreshing wind washing away cares
External awareness of God's awesomeness

Jack

Joyful breath of encouragement
Action in motion
Creative in word and work
Kindness an expression of his care

Judith

Just a ray of sunshine
Unashamed of sharing self
Daring you to be better
Inclusive of everyone
Teacher of yoga
Happy as a lark

Trump

Tragedy in the making
Running things to the ground
Uncontrolled in speaking lies
Murdering our sense of politeness
Peace of mind disturbed

Biden

Building up confidence
Increasing awareness
Demonstrating care for others
Emerging into a new era
Noticing what is important

Blake

Water

Wonderful refreshing
Amazingly restorative
Tasty refuel
Enriched energy
Real thirst quencher

Your Author

Edith Blake is a retired education administrative assistant who now uses her time and talents to serve her church and community. A local poet for 15 years, she hosted and participated in Open Mics throughout Hampton Roads. The author has been published in *Skipping Stones* Poetry Magazine and has composed two Advent Devotionals for her church, St. Andrew Lutheran, that include poetry, scripture and prayers. She released her first book <u>New Beginnings</u> in 2020, a collection of her own poetry and works from her passed husband, Bill.

Blake

<u>colophon</u>
Brought to you by Wider Perspectives Publishing, care of James Wilson, with the mission of advancing the poetry and creative community of Hampton Roads, Virginia.

See our production of works from ...

Chichi Iwuorie
Symay Rhodes
Tanya Cunningham-Jones
    (Scientific Eve)
Terra Leigh
Ray Simmons
Samantha Borders-Shoemaker
Bobby K.
    (The Poor Man's Poet)
J. Scott Wilson (TEECH!)
Charles Wilson
Gloria Darlene Mann
Neil Spirtas
Jorge Mendez & JT Williams
Sarah Eileen Williams
Stephanie Diana (Noftz)
the Hampton Roads
    Artistic Collective

Jason Brown (Drk Mtr)
Martina Champion
Tony Broadway

Zach Crowe
Ken Sutton
Crickyt J. Expression
Lisa M. Kendrick
Cassandra IsFree
Nich (Nicholis Williams)
Samantha Geovjian Clarke
Natalie Morison-Uzzle
Gus Woodward II
Patsy Bickerstaff
Catherine TL Hodges
Jack Cassada
Dezz

... and others to come soon.

We promote and support the artists of the 757
from the seats, from the stands,
from the snapping fingers andclapping hands
from the pages, and the stages
and now we pass them forth
to the ages

> Check for the above artists on FaceBook, the Virginia Poetry Online channel on YouTube, and other social media.

www.ingramcontent.com/pod-product-compliance
Lightning Source LLC
Chambersburg PA
CBHW031214090426
42736CB00009B/913